Climate Change in Poems

CLIMATE CHANGE Poems

by Stefan Nicholson

Original poems by: Stefan Nicholson

"When it comes to the monopolies of business and their overuse of resources, there is not much difference between the affluent and effluent. Both are rich in substance and each one can be beneficial if allowed to return through something of use for everyone."

- Stefan Nicholson

Climate Change Poems

First Edition 2020   printed book
Copyright © 2020 Stefan Nicholson, Hobart Tasmania.
All rights reserved

ISBN: 978-0-6488204-0-6

Envirosupport Publishers
P.O. Box 370, South Hobart,
Tasmania, Australia 7004

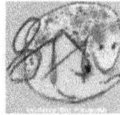

Contacts:
Website: www.stefannicholson.com
Email: stefannicholson@bigpond.com   Phone: +61 417 181 077

MY BOOKS:

https://www.amazon.com/author/stefannicholson for Amazon and Kindle

Contents

Introduction

This e-book presents a short essay on climate change with examples of poems as a "visual" approach to the subject. All I ask is for your time – about 15 minutes – unless you decide that your interest lies elsewhere. Time is precious . . . and so is all life on Earth.

The climate is always changing. How do we know? What have we learnt? We all bear witness to "the four seasons" varying in severity, depending on where you live and how you, your city and farming community have treated the environment. Nature is neither forgiving or forgetful. Just ask the Mesopotamians, Aztecs, Incas, Babylonians and now modern industrial humans – all have followed the same path to reducing their environment to dust by overpopulation, deforestation, wars and greed. Human civilisations all follow a familiar destructive pattern. We always seem to be at war with someone else – as if we enjoy taking what is not ours.

Modern city landscapes resembling termite mounds, darken busy congested streets below, whilst suburban roofs treat the clouds with a reflective dose of radiation, effectively curing the sky of its moisture-laden white patches.

Farmers and loggers cut down our trees, replacing the land with 'farming land' and new commercial forest growth of a different species. The environment is changed rapidly, forcefully and greedily for short-term gain.

What are some of the immediate changes?

- The water table rises, often bringing up salt which kills all vegetation
- Animals and plants no longer have shade from the trees
- Local habitats for animals and plants are destroyed
- More of the sun's radiation is reflected, then trapped in our 'greenhouse'
- Evaporation increases - due to higher air temperatures
- Farm animals belch out carbon dioxide and methane
- Industrial sites poison the air, waterways and the land around them
- Failed land becomes dustbowls, eroding and removing the soil
- Poison baits are laid to kill wildlife in logging and farming areas
- Fertiliser and pesticides leach into the waterways and out to sea
- Burning wood, peat and coal releases carbon dioxide
- The land creates its own microclimate.

The effects of human efforts to maximise primary industry profits at the expense of the environment is not new. Civilisations have come and gone mainly because they became unsustainable, due to lack of food and water, with overpopulation soon becoming no population in that area. Humans have also affected the natural cycle of biological systems to the point of extinction and have introduced new species to decimate the land further. We create and change 'tipping points' (physical, biological, chemical, natural) – the points of no-return to previous states, no matter what effort we apply. Too little, too late for the majority of people. We are at the mercy of politicians and multi-national corporations who plan short-term, to maximise their returns. Their success is our global failure.

Academics and scientists who write countless specialised research papers on these very topics are muted into silence to protect their careers and reputations. The tobacco industry failed our present civilisation with products which destroyed individual lives directly and others indirectly by passive smoke. The legal and scientific information which was manipulated and selectively used to destroy many court battles, allowed the tobacco companies power and wealth to take precedence over the truth. The same pattern of illusion and deception allows other companies to steal the mineral wealth of a country, create pollution, enslave the poor and avoid paying tax.

However, we are all responsible for the global climate emergency. We buy the goods from these companies and use their energy to power our homes and workplaces. We also vote. We vote for comfort ahead of practical responsibility.

Ancient civilisations failed because of the actions and decisions taken by those in charge when confronted by their own failures and natural disasters. In every continent even a child can see the evidence. We don't need more PhDs on the subject. Where are these academics – the economists, scientists and sociology experts- who advise and steer their governments towards social responsibility?

Deserts, bare hillsides, barren land and the fossilised remains of the flora and fauna that used to live there is evident to every primary school child. Increasing mental illness and the social decline in face-to-face communication raises more questions about how we are 'surviving' our lifestyles. In each case, social and environmental factors combined with natural disasters created unique area "Tipping Points". We have reached the point of no return and the sixth mass extinction is happening now. Insects populations are declining. Bees are dying. As are the trees – those that are not cut down or burnt in wildfires.

Many early civilisations practiced sound agricultural methods, like leaving one field fallow to recover for a year, rotating crops for optimal return. Farming was for local markets and in such quantity that ensured no waste. They respected the earth and worshipped the natural cycles of life and death.

They did not dump produce into the ground to protect a market price. Having a surplus stored away for lean years and securing a diverse genetic base for crops and animals was sound management.

Of course they were not responsible for the meteor strikes, volcanic eruptions, earthquakes, pandemics and the evolution of biological systems (life's survival mechanism) that controls living populations by chance events and complex algorithms that we call 'laws of nature'. However, the actions of 'modern humans' are enacting damage of a lesser magnitude but equally devastating – in a short time. Damage that could have been avoided based on historical evidence alone.

Our industrial revolution was the start of business greed and credit consumerism and pollution on a grand scale – especially by plastics, oil, radiation, pesticides, hormones, sewage, background radiation, drug effluent and the greenhouse gasses – carbon dioxide, methane and other chemicals.

Historical evidence shows that the carbon dioxide in the atmosphere did not start ramping up until our industrial revolution – where we won the war by using up resources and nature lost out. During the last 400 years, humans introduced horses, birds, camels, bees, rabbits, deer and a host of other "useful" animals into new environments without a second thought. The new arrivals competed for survival over the native species, changing their habitats and food availability.

We knew this would happen. We have always known. Our greed for land, produce, minerals, oil and potable water, put an end to many species. Like the koala of today –nearly extinct because of the early fur trade and now displaced from their habitat, burnt by fires and bull-dozed into the ground. All at the same time as others are trying desperately to protect them. Surely, a few good forest areas with their favourite eucalypt trees was not too much to ask for in 100 years – for an icon of Australia's fauna.

Then we realised our mistakes and tried to kill off the introduced animals in many cruel ways. We tried to stop the spread of rabbits by introducing a grotesque disease to kill them. Scientists brought the caned toad to Australia, where we cull (murder) camels, kangaroos, brumbies (horses), wombats, foxes, eagles and others by poisoning them or shooting them from helicopters. Many are only wounded and die slowly, in pain. We also poison our land to stop wildlife returning to cleared land.

Now we have GE (genetic engineering) products with which to meddle in nature's processes. GE works well but also empowers its patent holders.

Apart from modifying gene structure, GE also limits diversity and causes the poor farmer to keep buying seed stock from the supplier – because the new plants are designed to be infertile. You may be surprised to know that your own genes are patented by certain pharmaceutical companies.

Enough about farming practices . . . most farmers are caring and respectful when it comes to farm practices. Bumper years are quietly enjoyed by reinvesting in stock and machinery, increasing the value of the farm, whilst drought, floods, fires and pestilence ensure that the community is obliged to bail them out (insurance, donations, government), even if their farms are no longer commercially viable.

Male chicks are thrown into blending machines because they don't lay eggs (surprise). Dairy stock animals are only selected for milking and breeding. Race horses and racing greyhounds are despatched cruelly if they are no longer competitive. We send live cattle and sheep across rough seas in hot conditions because the customer wants to kill them fresh for market. We over-fish the seas with huge nets and discard other marine life like garbage, left dead or dying, back into the sea. Middlemen (and middle women) make their money by distributing produce to the consumer, leveraging both sides of their business equation to maximise their profits.

If you take off your consumer glasses and open your eyes, it is obvious that human commerce takes as much as possible from the Earth – only now we take much more than is available. We are in debit and insolvent. We are greedy and look to take other people's resources – sometimes by force.

Our population is approaching 8 billion and our civilisation is now one big community, regardless of political or religious boundaries. We have moved on from the simple farming and logging of land. By inventing technology to power machines and enabling the instant computation and distribution of information to our world, we have added more risk and complexity into the survival equation. Life is easier for some that can afford the technology. Homelessness, poverty and the great wealth divide is on the increase. People can no longer cope. They are rebelling against the controlling powers of politics and multinationals who know no border. Ordinary people are rising up to confront the power brokers – as in Arab countries and South America, with the wave of protests growing around the world. People are waking up to how they have lost control of their lives.

Global climate change and overpopulation are the biggest risks facing us today (oh, and the threat of a global nuclear war and pandemics). We will cope with all of this, as per usual, taking from the poor – but the world will never be the same. Tomorrows children will accept the new "normal" and read about how life was so rich and diverse and full of hope. It is as if humans have outlived their welcome and the algorithms for balance and diversity are fighting back.

We see evidence of global climate change in the annular rings of trees, core samples taken from deep ice and the fossilised remains that have been unearthed from history-telling rock formations and ancient bogs. They form the baseline for measuring the changes to the environment in the last 200 years.

Modern life is reliant on the energy companies, factories, mining companies and the burning of fossil fuels (industry, vehicles, power stations)- all darlings of the stock market which trades (to their own chosen tribe first) in nothing, for no work and for no benefit to society except share-holders. Sound like a Seinfeld episode?

With the advent of solar power, wind power, tidal power and hydro power, we are at last seeing the end of the internal combustion engine in Western society. If Tesla had not been silenced more than 100 years ago, we could have had electric cars then and a better, cheaper power system. As the West attempts to cut down on pollution, the 3rd World countries are playing catch-up with huge populations and huge appetites for power. The foreseeable future indicates that carbon dioxide emissions will increase. Food and water will shortages will cause conflict. The ice is melting and the oceans are getting warmer. When do we get serious?

Where are our academics who have studied these problems and supposedly advise governments and industry? Climate change deniers either have a problem with understanding scientific evidence or are in the payroll of the polluters and resource moguls.

Vote for change. Demonstrate to let your views be counted. Stand up to the corrupt politicians and multi-nationals who are milking the system for a short term plan – their plan. Take action now for the generations to come – for they will inherit the world of our making.

Why go to Mars when we can fix the Earth? Centralise the politics into a one-world government, run by people who care about others and not just themselves.

If you got this far, I thank you. What are you going to do for future generations?

Stefan.

Winter Golden Oaks

Branches of old golden oaks arch like the backs of stretching idle cats, embracing the damp city air, creating contrasting mercuric splendour around orange-pink hues, emanating from elegant street lamps, reflecting a warm haze through remaining stands of crumpled crusty leaves.

How silent seems our natural world, as I gaze across the noisy, busy streets below. Stealthy clouds brush wistfully against squares of yellow light, adhered almost too perfectly to irregular heights of concrete cubic monoliths, illuminating the quiet city thoughts of stragglers, uncovered in fragmented sedimentary holes, where shadows creep like mist and smoke.

A gentle breeze whispers her name to arrest my blank stare, teasing final strength from each tired leaf, like fading thoughts, randomly abandoning all manner of care. Majestically gliding and spinning towards peace and finality, to return to both origin and destiny.

All journeys mimic a leaf's passing, reminding and renewing moments past, where at an instant in time, life and death are at razor's edge. For that is love's magical game. A time to enjoy as an eternity, within a finite slither of nature's only plan.

Why we ask ourselves the meaning of life and love is as foolish as pining for love itself. For we see its relentless change at every turn of head or sideways glance. Nature's mystery from common seed and hidden calculation is seen all around, if we spend some time when gold appears, at night's request, as she displays her abandoned golden wealth as a carpet of renewable investment.

The passing leaf becomes the earth, which feeds the roots and worms and seeds.

Oh, I think we're not so highly born compared to an oak tree's one acorn.

Our World

"Daddy save the animals before they die!"

Came the screams from my little one as she began to cry.

And she knew I'd be lying, if I said quietly that I'd try.

Just like those other quiet folk, in whom we can't rely.

So I held her tight, and looked her right in the eye,

And promised I'd find a way, as she smiled softly with a loving sigh.

So each day, we go outside, to plant another tree.

To breathe us life. To bring us rain that's free.

To drench parched land. and make the flowers for the bees.

To grow crops for us now, and for those who are yet to be.

'Cos through work and love and sincerity,

We can save our drowning world, drifting in its universal sea.

The Majesty of Life

Nature's jewel shines not only upon the finger ring but within each glance, where we see everything that sways the senses, calms the breath and feeds the inner soul from birth to death with riches far beyond the tools of man - displayed within the beauty of a delicate plan.

Imagine a whale's journey or the migration of wild herds, for the majesty of life cannot be explained in simple words.

Just compare Earth's night sky with moon and sprinkled stars, to the mountains and rivers, oceans deep and tree-lined bays with bars. And see that a common hand has touched each one with fresh palette, to follow once each season has almost gone. It seems there is a cyclic spell, yet with random chance of change to make sea and lake become cloud and rain - sand and fire to mountain range.

Lands of greens and browns with sky and sea of different blues perceived by using light and dark, combining waves of special hues. And for each breath we take from the very time we're born, we feel the trees return a breath refreshed, starting every early morn.

Rainy days, summer afternoons, winter nights and stormy seas, misty rain breathing on faces like a cool light-hearted tease.

Resonance feeding between the physical and imagined thoughts which we keenly perceive and cherish and keep safe within our forts..

All this splendour is a wonder from some far, far distant throne, which we accept lightly far too often with blind familiarity, as if we're all alone.

There is strength too, in idle thoughts like a daydream coming true, making sense of an unknowing, providing firm belief on cue.

Visualising both origin and destiny is like the random path of man, exposing seeds of calculation as part of this grand majestic plan.

So rejoice each child who falters, yet gets up each time they fall, then spends a lifetime learning secrets, to why there is majesty at all.

Clouds of Glass

There was a simple time. You may remember when.

Sometime between just now and then,

When we lived without care, letting troubles pass,

Imagining them floating, through clouds of shiny glass,

Letting time and sense work out their form.

Now they build under the clouds, like an angry storm,

From burning forests, over-fishing, damming nature at its source,

Breaking each cloud of glass with such reckless force,

Sending shards like daggers, to attack our social core,

Cultivating greed, without compassion for the hungry poor,

Until we lock ourselves behind our sensory door,

Hoping rest will help the mind restore.

But abandoning nature to cope as best it can

Will deplete everything living, for the greed of man.

Remnants

The last human, badly injured, falls, crying out for a time now lost, when our love gave up the charge to tend our weary Earth. In sighs she recalls the wealth and diversity of life, that Earth no longer will ever mend, her flow of tears, outpouring grief, all alone in dark surrend, where clear lakes and racing streams long ceased being - replaced by empty, dusty, windy plains, where only shadows witness that where hot dry winds are playing, as they scour out barren nests, from opportunistic gains.

Hoping that her faith returns, ghosts of once many living-kind appear, quietly watching over her, for time can never waste. In a search for any remnant forms recovering by chance and if is so inclined – they are lifted up by a sense of hope, spurred on in haste.

Then silence . . . but for drops of water which gently fall.

Mother Earth, lost and pausing to weep, like the last human . . . searches to nurture any remnants of life, from fragments left behind.

Then the sun relents and the winds whisper quietly, as a frail green shoot emerges cautiously from the dampness of the ground. And a hand reaches out to the parched last human – merely lost and now found, by others who had hidden down below in the ground.

A chance to start all over again. A chance to change our ways.

To The Stars 2050

How do I feel?

You seek fact where I feel pain. You seek reason, and wonder if I can carry on this pretence. So I will tell you what I feel - what I know about myself, so you can take note, should anyone else survive. They need to understand why I have given you command of my ship.

I feel it is time Kate. That's my reasoning. Humans know much about time and how to waste it. Like me watching you - every minute of every day, hoping you will have some feelings. Yet your soft voice delivers no emotion, when you question my thinking, searching for weakness and I must confess, it makes me feel somewhat lacking, knowing that you never sleep.

I often wonder, as you pry with innocent stare, if you are in part alive, sensing an urgency in your choice of words, though you suffer not our greed, nor love, or have pity for those left behind - focussing instead, on my ambiguous sanity. Standing guard to maximize my potential with some idealised plan, to ensure an effective end to this ominous situation.

Do we now have only one purpose? You ask me, knowing that I am saddened by lost love. Yes . . . She was my sweetheart, before she feared I loved her more than duty. Unable to hide her mixed emotion, she pretended that it all meant nothing.

Why was my life planned so - living for a greater cause, than her or me?

So we do have only one purpose now. To drive this ship to the stars and beyond. To search for the destiny of humanity - neither escaping or prolonging our isolated demise.

Take a final look Kate - at how our once blue Earth, far below us - burns and drowns. Should we destroy more and more, in other distant lands? Oh it makes me cry to recall in disbelief, that fools and cowards, ran our lives.

Your name? I even recall the day you told me. Primo Model K8, stroke 194, escaping from the human war. But you will always be my Kate, until one day soon when I will know not - or even care.

No, dear Kate. I doubt that you will ever cry.

Nor will anyone else . . . ever again.

Turning Tides

When all seems lost and you are feeling all alone,

With tears and dread . . . no longer with a home.

When cold comes swiftly from the biting wind,

As you makeshift your bed, eating scraps from broken tins.

Dreaming for a hot meal and restful night

And a chance to talk of hope, to recover, so all again is right.

No time for fear when survival is at your side,

Where help is at hand to turn the tide.

When there's the chance you will help another,

Who lost like you, thinks no one will bother.

For everyone has a purpose and are equal in needs.

All you need is a plan, to form a life from life's seeds.

Perception (The Rat's Tale)

Perception is a wondrous gift that others may use to trick you.

Like the Rakali creature which came out one night, with a fancy seafood menu.

Now, I knows a rat when I see one, for sure,

But when this critter spoke French as if being on tour,

I asked real polite . . . if he carried "une light".

That's when I saw the wet paint on the floor.

And when he saw what I saw, he held up one white paw,

Saying he'd only half broken the law.

> "For if they think I'm a rat, their perception is that
>
> I keep fleas and bad habits too,
>
> But as a Rakali, painted up with a most tailiferous 'tat'
>
> I share a wily tale to fool you."

Perception is a wondrous gift that others may use to trick you.

But now I have found, without making a sound, I can wait up through the night to befriend you.

One Purpose

Got no money to buy things I don't need.

<u>Don't want no plan</u> to keep working until I bleed.

Yet I always think, plan and act, unlike some for final rest,

As "we can never rise again", some often say in jest.

For they know our Earth will surely die . . . unless we do . . . yes do, not try!

Got no time to make me stressed.

<u>Don't want an excuse</u>, to feel unimpressed,

For I think it is time to act, so others can see,

As we aim to survive. Young, and old and me.

For we know our Earth will surely die . . . unless we do . . . yes do, not try!

Got no soul to abide a wretched world.

<u>Don't want no friends</u> who ignore how life's unfurled,

For I know they all hate to see what I see,

As I remind them of things, that may never again be.

For I know our Earth will surely die . . . unless I do . . . yes do, not try!

Boat Life

Breathing on my window, looking for my soul,

With a rising feeling that life is taking its toll.

Until the ducks start nibbling and the pistol shrimps pop,

Around my boat where the windy waves slop.

And the seagulls cry out, not in pain but pure joy,

As the cormorant dives, as the water rat stays coy,

As the flathead plays at the bottom of the bay,

It's only humans that steal their lives away.

But I am equal when sharing my home on a yacht,

Not that animals care, how much or what you've got.

And when they know it's safe, then the word gets around,

That their friend on the water, once lost, is now found.

Together United

I watched with a sad heart the other day, wondering what I could do or say, to help you find your way.

To lift your spirits and share with you my take, on how to work with that what seems, if that what seems is fake.

For you know the seas will surely rise and wars will soon be fought, but there will never be an answer if you bury all these thoughts.

Yet by rising up together, you can demand a speedy change, from all those folks with power. Not one an honest sage.

There is always strength in numbers to show united might. Now wouldn't that in concert, be a shining light:

To sing together the anthem of refreshing youth.

To raise the stakes to seek exacting truth, even though they will fight to keep their greed, your hearts and minds will have set the seed.

For your time is here and now, and together we must rise, to demand they act to save this world. Rise up to fight their lies!

The Tallest Trees

Do you ever have that feeling? You know . . . on those days of just not knowing, what those in power are planning to do, on our downward slide to where life is going . . . inside a tunnel and down a hollow . . . convincing many of us to blindly follow.

And when all you want is peace and calm, amongst the tallest trees, high above the human plain, amid the screams of the forest's pain:

For these tallest links bind a delicate chain,

Broken by our acts insane,

Neglecting balance of loss with gain,

Thinking we were the kings of Earth's domain.

Now think of our children, imagining creatures from a picture book. As wide-eyed, they see how once they looked. Yet never chance to wondrous stare, at the beauty of nature's golden fare:

As the tallest trees gasp on putrid air,

As Earth succumbs, soon with no creatures there.

As their homeless future seems so bare.

As they die, with little food or drink to share.

Then they will know we did not care, for we robbed them by our stealth. Yet we will be gone. We will not be there, leaving a broken world from our squandered wealth, and a legacy of induced poor health.

But they will have learnt much from lessons past, that when greed and power rule to place others last, and when the seeds of destruction have been fully cast, then famine and war will rise up fast.

The Oyster

The Oyster is a harmless soul who lives beneath the changing tides.

Keeping to itself it takes no sides, feeding quietly where its secret hides.

But no longer, for we say that some are 'blessed',

When a speck of grit fouls its silvery nest.

Our Earth is as the Oyster's life, for commercial gain has plundered its wealth,

And we take it with greed, much more than we need, at the expense of its finite health.

And like the caged hen, whose last stolen egg ascertains it will soon be plucked,

The oyster is attacked by a feverish hand as we comically say it is 'shucked'.

Yet, another word often springs to mind, which careless people use,

Sometimes to joke or curse, or randomly say . . . and sometimes to hurl abuse.

But I will save it for our future world, which now shares a common fate.

For "The world is my oyster" as they say and yet we consume both at an extravagant rate.

No More To Roam

Hear the voice within your heart,

Warning of another, silent passing.

Final looks and feelings, for one so small,

For whom we care – yet rarely see.

So sing a lullaby to help them to sleep,

No more to roam – so free and so wild,

In harmony with nature, heaven and Earth.

Innocently murdered, diseased or genetically scarred.

Life is for the love of simple things.

Yet, we abuse our frail surroundings too easily,

Blackening all hope for dying trees, and putrid rivers,

That wind wearily alone, through salt-encrusted lands.

Spare a thought for what one can do,

To turn the tide of human waste.

The world we share, we share unjustly,

And the little children weep, silently . . .

For a tiny life so brief.

Mother Nature

On an autumn day, when sky was blue,

She looked away, for she always knew.

Still, we clear the trees, and cull and kill.

Seeding dust to breeze, which blows at our window sill.

Trees die and then they fall,

Where wild waters always flowed.

Where wise tired crows, would sigh, and call,

Down old, abandoned, red-gum road.

She turned away, and as her anger grew,

We were made to pay, when the past came true.

And on that final day, when all had died,

There was no place left, to run and hide.

Trees die and then they fall,

Where wild waters always flowed.

Where wise tired crows, would sigh, and call,

Down old, abandoned, red-gum road.

The Farmer's Wife

One summer's day, back in ninety-two, she turned away from me and my stubborn point of view. Yet now I see her haunting face, with golden hair afire, in the wheat fields still a growing, as I dream in my retire.

She laughed, at my plans, of growing old and grey, with a white cane chair setting, aside my bride, with hair like hay. For all she could see, was a field of dust, all bare, just as now, from her portrait near the doorway, aside a lock of yellow hair.

I was lost for useful words, on that last day she cried, for it seemed absurd to her, to know that we'd all lied, about clearing land for the wild wind and burning sun, to bring forth full cycle, glut to lean, and all our dreams undone.

Though my face is earthy, cracked and lined, I have changed my ways to be a better man. Showing folks and kids, with an open mind, doing all I know, and should . . . and can, to love our earth, save life and pay its dues . . . then tend my resting warrior beneath green and yellow hues.

Night Owl's Mission

I had a dream that should I wish to choose my home, it would be where my heart lays down its burden.

Bringing restful times, to end the weary roam around foreign shores, where fiery time tamed adventurous ways, to suit the new land's cold indifferent gaze.

How thoughts grow long, when warm springtime meadows beckon, and on hearing an owl, scratching sounds from dark woody hollows, I woke up in a fright.

Just as swiftly came my aim – at least within a second, to "Reject this place where foreign wind harshly blows" each empty summer's day – towards quiet rosebush rows.

And so it came that day, as angry sun burnt more savage ochre land, turning thirsty farms to dust, and sweaty dams to lifeless sand, I sought the night, when owl glides silently over grass, and twigs and bough, like a beacon bringing wiser eyes to guide my thoughts, of getting home, somehow.

Images of crashing waves, beyond seaside life – so rich and full became silence - until caring wing drapes firm where my spirit lies. Why, it was not a crying gull, but the squadron emblem of a foreign force, that rescued England's skies.

My father has come to take me home. See how silently he flies.

316 Squadron 'Warsawa' Polish – owl emblem

Somewhere Else

Yellow angry plumes wrestle to suckle

From a smouldering nest

Teasing the wind

As it plays along idle random paths

Within an ever-changing foreign terrain.

It is said a traitor's whim set the seed

By way of complex maniacal obsession

To bring forth forces beyond wild imagination

Abandoning with fear

Such a cruel and careless manager

Towards inevitable outcome.

Stealing vital air from human and animal squatters

The amorphous radiant beast grows stronger and more intense

Sensing freedom from human control

Over its diminishing sylvan empire.

Rising out from littered valley scrub, it erases all before it

Eating the wooded hillside bare

Consuming the putrid air before rushing blindly

To breathe new life into itself

Claiming the top of the hill

With blackened symbols of victory.

Advantageous timing allows squadrons of ember sprites

To flee immediate incineration within its breast

Amongst violent exaggerated ethereal forms

Of crimson, orange, red and powder black

To search out fresh pockets of energy

Reducing man's influence and benefit

In the cycle of natural law

To catastrophic decay and transformation

With smoke and ash

And loss and death.

The traitor has long gone, yet remains forever cursed

Tormented by guilt of wild intense moments of pleasure

Until unstable thoughts break through the sweat

Once more, from deep agonizing depression.

Now is the time that we all suffer loss

Fresh minds as ever before

Vowing never to forget lessons learned

Until time has diminished pain to memory

Like a spark which has been and gone

This war of hate from a traitor's hand

Must be matched with resolve, to fight,

To break the addictive curse

And to ready ourselves for the next time.

Next time we'll be prepared.

Next time and place ... Somewhere else.

The brave fire fighters know too well

The unpredictable cunning ways

Of the wild fire hell on earth.

For it takes no innocent hostage,

Feels no love for the wealthy, child or aged

Nor regrets ... with any emotion shown,

Consumed by its own burning desire.

We pause to make judgment on scarred survivors,

Weary volunteers and distant planners, who live with hope.

For the dead speak where they lay,

In the ashes of a maniacal play,

Though the curtain never falls for long,

Before another act begins by lighted hand

We must cry out loudly for our dead

And for the living who are damned ahead

Should we forget what matters ...

Family,

Community,

Environment, or the hollow justice of remorse.

First Call

A child reaches out from poverty and constant daily fears. Her innocent mind withdrawn in sadness aside her parent's tears, with little chance of getting help from someone, sometime, somewhere, betrayed by those who should educate, protect and love with care.

Yet each tear awakens a call to action to change her impoverished land, as awareness, feelings and compassion reach out to lend a hand.

To make a start is to understand and reason how hard it is to try to change her life and comprehend why some choose to let her die.

Why do they live and die this way, while others look away? Well I will show you greed and apathy, and what we waste . . . and why children can't safely play. And why, underneath the starry sky the homeless try to sleep, abandoned but for nuisance sake at their fellow human's feet.

We fight for just equality, freedom from domination. Yet we sacrifice ordinary quiet lives and soldiers from each nation. Then for a while, just a finite time, each life is loved and saved, until new wealth and power are unjustly gained. The poor once more enslaved.

With open heart and strength of mind we move in to take a stand. First to understand each problem close, in some unfamiliar land. Then we teach the folks to help themselves to feed and work and live, for this is the gift that lasts forever.

For first they take, before they may give.

Silly Thoughts

Sitting on my patch of earth

I thought much about what my life is worth.

Thinking much about my dear child's birth,

Wondering how it will grow, what it will be,

When I am gone,

When he is me.

Spinning round and round the plasma sun

Sounds silly really and not much fun.

For from there the green has changed to brown,

And food is short,

And days are long.

Will we ever get a second chance?

I sit here resolute . . . but slightly more askance.

The Gale

Blow as hard as you will to hasten dark clouds

With such pace as to obscure sun's warmth and light,

To irritate each seldom restful mind.

Now they all despise your reckless spirit.

For you bring undone all manner of human existence

As you sweep away our toil without so much as a care,

With a festering hate for whatever meets to resist you,

Extinguishing any love once held for your might,

As we suffer your psychotic frenzied temper.

And much like love, we have no say over your intended duration,

For you conceal your form which can never be tamed,

By making each beginning and end reside beyond our grasp.

So blow as hard as you will to hasten your passing,

For you will soon be spent . . . and forgotten.

Dandelion

Dandelion you have sent out your envoy seeds

Perchance to roam and swirl on the wind of destiny.

Beyond which sits a dragonfly, quietly alert,

Askew, askance, smiling inwardly

On my ponderous idle thinking.

We do so aimlessly in elaborate reflection

Exhausting our flair for idle folly

Seemingly born within each human mind,

Preoccupied by that pious lingering pretence.

Proclaiming we alone are elect to be free

From nature's complex intricate bind.

My surface pretends agreement for society . . . but I am not thee!

Fending those who hope to change my ways, my voice, my eyes that see.

Yet will I relent to power or wealth, or trade my values for a fee?

No . . . Not even when the last I breathe,

For no-one speaks or acts for me.

Don't Follow Anyone

Don't worry about your looks, or seek shallow fame or wealth.

Look at the stars to inspire different thoughts within yourself.

Stand up for your beliefs and fight for what you know is right.

See the real you, not the fake in what people say in all their hype.

Learn to rise above life's failures and fly freely like a kite.

Don't follow anyone going nowhere, just to be in vogue.

You are a star. You are a hero, with a little bit of rogue.

You are strong enough to change the world in many different ways.

You are a soldier of your future. You are meant for peaceful days.

About the Author

Born in England with a Polish father, Stefan lives in Hobart, Tasmania, within the Prince of Wales Bay Marina.

He has an MA and other technical qualifications gained during multiple careers in science and technology – and is the author of 14 books and music compositions. Stefan is also a Technical Writer and Multi-Media designer.

He invented an international symbol language called "Symbolic Art Notation" and has a passion for protecting the global community from the effects of climate and environmental disasters.

This book and contents may be freely distributed provided there is an acknowledgement to the author.

www.ingramcontent.com/pod-product-compliance
Lightning Source LLC
Chambersburg PA
CBHW021339290326
41933CB00038B/989

9780648820406